Manufactured by Amazon.ca
Bolton, ON

44845096R00061